Now that you are
Born Again

PASTOR YEMISI BAMGBOSE

NOW THAT YOU ARE BORN AGAIN

Copyright © Pastor Yemisi Bamgbose
Winners' Way
Redeemed Christian Church of God
Worship Centre: Westgate House,
2nd Floor, South Wing, Spital Street
Dartford, Kent DA1 2EH.
Email: Winnersway@btinternet.com
Website: www.winnersway.org.uk

This edition is published April 2010

First Edition

Published by Roots
The Old Rectory
Springhead Road
Northfleet
DA11 8HN
01474 338724
www.rootsmarketingltd.com

Contents

Foreward

"There was a man of the Pharisees, named Nicodemus, a ruler of the Jews; The same came to Jesus by night, and said unto Him, Rabbi, we know that Thou art a teacher come from God: for no man can do these miracles that Thou doest, except God be with him. Jesus answered and said unto him, Verily, verily, I say unto thee, Except a man be born again, he cannot see the Kingdom of God".

Nicodemus said to him, How can a man be born when he is old? Can he enter the second time into his mother's womb, and be born? Jesus answered, verily, verily I say unto thee Except a man be born of water and the spirit, he cannot enter the kingdom of God.

John 3:1-5

Meditate on the words of Jesus, to see the kingdom of God you need to be born again and to enter the kingdom of God you need to be born of water and of the spirit.

John 3:5.

Now that you are born again is a book that will guide you through your new journey and walk in Christ and I pray that as you read this booklet, it will help you start well and build a firm foundation.

This is thanking the Almighty God for making this booklet possible and I hope it will bless you as you read and begin to understand you are now a member of an outstanding family.

Welcome into the Household of God!

Now That You Are Born Again

BEING BORN AGAIN is a term used to describe any person who has just surrendered his or her life to the Lord Jesus. This individual must have resolved in his or her heart to forget their former ways of life to follow the Lord Jesus. Having repented of all sins, giving their absolute and total life to the Lord Jesus. There are things that this person needs to know about his or her new found faith in order to be grounded in God.

Although salvation is free but it costs God His Son, and there are steps to follow and decisions to be taken as you begin this journey of self discovery. Giving your life to Jesus Christ is the best experience that can happen to you and in this I congratulate you and welcome you into the family of God. Jesus will help you as you begin this life transforming walk with Him. This journey requires your totality because it is a long haul walk and not a short one at all. As you take a step He is there by your side supporting you and holding you up and you will not fall or slip from His hands in Jesus name.

Now that your name has been written in the Lamb's book of life, there are things you'll need to know about your new found faith and what to do as to how your name will not be wiped away from that book of life. There are principles that guide every child of God in this new life. This principle will help you to be grounded and to grow daily in the Lord.

Step 1

NUMBER ONE THING you'll need to do is to share your salvation experience with your friends and family members. Matthew 10:32 says, *'Therefore whosoever confesses Me before men, him I will also confess before My Father who is in heaven'.*

Mark 8:38 says *'For whosoever is ashamed of Me and My words in this adulterous and sinful generations, of him the Son of Man also will be ashamed when He comes in the glory of His Father with the Holy Angels".*

In Romans 10:10 that says *'For with heart one believes to righteousness, and with the mouth confession is made to salvation'.*

From the above scriptures, it is important to share your new found faith with your loved ones.

Step 2

YOU WILL NEED TO BE PART of a living church, where the word of God is preached and taught undiluted. In such an environment your faith will be anchored properly upon the solid foundation of Christ and the principles of the bible.

Acts 2 verse 41 to 42 says "*Then they that gladly received His word were baptised, and the same day there were added unto them about three thousand souls. And they continued steadfastly in the apostles doctrine and fellowship, and in breaking of bread and in prayers*".

Hebrews 10:25 says "*Not forsaking the assembly of ourselves together, as the manner of some is, but exhorting one another, and so much the more, as ye see the day approaching*".

When you are part of a local church, you become part of a big family of God, your spiritual progress can be managed by the follow-up team. You will have someone to help you grow daily, pray for you and you will be encouraged to be part of a house fellowship. There are so many advantages of becoming part of a local church. You will be able to ask questions at Bible study, learn how to pray better. You will also be taught how to hear from God and how to exercise your faith.

Proverb 27 verse 17 says "*iron sharpeneth iron, so a man sharpeneth the countenance of his friend*" so there are many benefits and blessings attached to becoming part of a local

Step 3

YOU WILL NEED TO HAVE A BIBLE where you can have access to the written word of God. There are different versions of the bible-Living Bible, King James Version, New King James Version, New International standard, New American standard etc. Carefully choose the one that will enable you to understand the message fully. Or if you can afford to buy more than one version of the Bible in order to give fuller and better interpretations.

You will need to study your Bible daily, as it is the word that will enable you to grow daily in the Lord.

2 Timothy 2:15 says, *'Study to show yourself approved unto God, a workman needed not be ashamed, but rightly dividing the word of truth.'*

The Bible also says, you will know the truth, and the truth will set you free. God will speak to you when you study His word. You can only know God through the knowledge of His word.

You will be able to know better the Person of Jesus Christ, the Holy Spirit and His Ministry to saints.

Since the Bible is God's complete revelation according to Colossians 1:25-27. The Bible is the guideline and manual of every believer in Jesus Christ as it reveals Christ's message of hope and eternal life. The Bible also demonstrates how christians should behave and comport themselves daily as we interact with people.

Since the Bible is the written word of God, you can only know God through His word, you will know your rights in Him and also know His blessings and your inheritance in Him. There are lessons to be learnt from the Bible and pitfalls to avoid when you study.

Anytime you want to study the word of God, you will need the help of the Holy Spirit, because He is the author of the Bible and He can enable you to understand the message better and also assist you to comprehend the intended message to you and open your understanding better.

In studying the Bible, it will be advisable to have a notebook, where you will write every thought that comes to your mind as you study, memory verses and prayer points as you go along

For every new believer, you will need to start reading the Bible from the New Testament; especially the book of John as it was there that Jesus spoke about Himself and His Mission when He was physically present here on earth. He spoke plainly about His Father, Himself, The Holy Spirit and Our eternal home (Heaven)
.

Read from the book of John to Matthew, Mark and Luke and there on to the book of Revelation. Memorise scriptures on a daily basis as this will help you to remember God's promises in the Bible and you can use it as a weapon against the devil and evil thoughts. Take time to study the entire Bible from Genesis to Revelation.

The word of God is the weapon of our warfare, as we cannot use physical weapons of bows and arrows to fight evil thoughts or spirits but the Word of God can counteract and destroy them.

In 2 Corinthians 10:4 the Bibles says *"For the weapons of our warfare are not carnal but mighty in God to the pulling down of strongholds".*

Step 4

YOU WILL NEED TO BE BAPTISED IN WATER by immersion. This is very important as it is the public declaration of your new found faith in Christ Jesus. The book of Mark 16:16 says, *'He who believes and is baptised will be saved, but he who does not believe is condemned.*

Romans 6:3-4 says, *'or do you not know that as many of us as were baptised into Christ Jesus were baptised into His death? Therefore we were buried with Him through baptism into death, that just as Christ was raised from the dead by the glory of the Father, even so we also should walk in newness of life'*

In some churches there is a special class for new converts; it varies from one church to another. In some they have believers class and baptismal class. From these classes, you will graduate into a workers class, before serving the Lord in your local church.

Step 5

BAPTISM IN THE HOLY SPIRIT is very crucial in order for you to be empowered and equipped for the journey ahead of you. In Mark 16:17 *'And these signs will follow those who believe; in My name they cast out demons; they will speak with new tongues'.* The new tongues come as a sign of the indwelling of the Holy Spirit.

The book of Acts 19:6 says; *'And when Paul had laid hands on them, the Holy Spirit came upon them, and they spoke with tongues and prophesied'. In John 14:26 that says "But the helper, the Holy Spirit, whom the Father will send in My name, He will teach you all things and bring to your remembrance all things that I said to you".*

In John 16:13 the Holy Spirit is also referred to as the Spirit of truth. In Luke 11:13 Jesus says *"If you then being evil know how to give good gift to your children, how much more will your heavenly father give the Holy Spirit to those who ask Him".*

Step 6

YOU WILL HAVE TO CHANGE your former habit, since being born again is not a physical experience but a spiritual experience, according to 2 Corinthians 5:17 '*Therefore, if any man is in Christ Jesus he is a new creature, old things have passed away behold all things have become new*' there will be a need for you to change your former ways of life to the new life in Christ Jesus and also to find a good mentor, e.g. as Paul mentored Timothy. You need someone that would be there and available to counsel and pray along with you until you are firmly grounded in the word of God'.

Step 7

PRAYER IS VERY CRUCIAL to a believer as water is crucial to a fish. It is a universal language between that individual and heaven, prayer shows our total dependency on God alone and not on our own abilities to make things happen for us. Cultivate the habit of prayer - Morning devotions Mark 1:35, Evening prayer Mark 6:46 and All night prayer Luke 6:12.

Attend a regular prayer meeting in your local church and ask the Holy Spirit to teach you on how to pray. 1 Thessalonians 5:17 says *'Pray without ceasing'.*

Luke 6:12 says *"Now it came to pass in those days that He went out to the mountain to pray, and continued all night in prayer and fasting".*

Step 8

DAILY LIVE A LIFE OF OBEDIENCE TO GOD and enlist His help on your daily endeavours. Remember you are now a new creation, old things have passed away, behold all things have become new. Let your conduct speak of a new found experience. If you have been a liar before, ask God for the grace to always speak the truth at all times. Let your watch word now be Holiness as 1 Peter 1:13 -16 says *'Therefore gird up the loins of your mind, be sober and be rest your hope fully upon the grace that is to be brought to you at the revelation of Jesus Christ. As obedient children not conforming yourselves to the former lust, as in your ignorance, but as He who called you is holy you also be holy in all your conduct. Because it is written, be holy for I am holy'*,

Isaiah 1:19 says *'if you are willing and obedient you will eat the good of the land'.*

For you to please and enjoy God, you must live a life of total obedience to Him and His word.

Step 9

LEARN TO GIVE YOURSELF TO THE SERVICE OF GOD and give your substance unto Him as well. You must pay your tithes and give your offering unto God. In Malachi 3: 10 -11says *"Bring all the tithes into the storehouse, That there may be food in My house, And prove Me now in this; Says the Lord of Hosts, If I will not open the windows of heaven, and pour out for you such blessing that there will not be room enough to receive it".*

Ecclesiastes 9:10 says *'Whatever your hand find to do, do it with all your might for there is no work or device or knowledge or wisdom in the grave',* 1 Corinthians 4:2 says *'More over it is required in stewards that one be found faithful'.*

You must serve God faithfully and with a right motive.

Step 10

CULTIVATE THE HABIT OF REGULAR FASTING, Paul admonishes us to give ourselves to fasting and prayer 1 Corinthians 7:5b, Matthew 17:21 *'However, this kind does not go out except by prayer and fasting'* learn to fast at least once a week.

Fasting helps you to develop your spiritual muscles and it will also move you from the natural realm into the spiritual realm. It also helps you to hear God more clearly and effectively as you devote yourself to prayer and fasting.

Step 11

YOU WILL NEED TO DEVELOP ABSOLUTE FAITH in God and in His words. *Without faith, no one can please God, for he who comes to God must believe that He is and that He is a rewarder of those who diligently seek Him,* Hebrews 11:6. If you are trusting God for anything , you will need faith to get it done. Anytime you believe the word of God, you are empowered to experience its reality.

As a new believer, you will need to know that nothing will work without faith in God. Nothing empowers like faith. It is faith that transports your miracle from the spiritual realm into the realm of reality.

Step 12

YOU MUST ALWAYS LIVE a life of thanksgiving unto God and be a testifier of His grace and mercy. Tell people of His mercy towards you and your family. Be a true witness for Him and He will prove Himself faithful unto you. Luke 17:17 -18 *'So Jesus answered and said were there not ten cleansed? But where are the nine? Were there not any found who returned to give glory to God except this foreigner?'* 1 Thessalonians 5:18 *'In everything give thanks, for this is the will of God in Christ Jesus for you'.*

Above all as a new born babe, you will need to desire the sincere milk of God (1 Peter 2:2). Cultivate a daily prayer time of 30 minutes or more. Take time to know the attributes of God through His word and obey all His teachings. Submit yourself to a godly leader that will be able to direct and mentor you aright.

Sincerely desire the gifts of the Holy Spirit and pray for the fruit of the Holy Spirit, which is a sign of maturity in Christ Jesus. Obey the leaders over you. Hebrews 13:17 says *'Obey those who rule you, and be submissive, for they watch out for your souls, as those who must give account. Let them do so with joy and not with grief, for that would be unprofitable for you'.*

Always remember to attend regular fellowships with other Christians.

You will need to remember that the devil does not give in or surrender to anyone except the power of God. Therefore you should leave religion for the the reality of the Kingdom of God.
The power of God in you will give your life value to your redemption reality. The Devil will try His absolute best to try and lure you back to your former ways of life, but you must always arm yourself with the word of God daily in order to quench the fiery darts of the enemy. James 4:7 *"Therefore submit to God. Resist the Devil and he will flee from you".*

Your life must have the expression of God's power. Salvation is not identity but a change of status from a sinner to a saint. It is an elevation of your status according to John 1:12 that says *"But as many as received Him, to them he gave right to become children of God, to those who believe in His name".*

May the Grace of God keep you secured and grounded to the end. Be Blessed. Shalom!